The Prayer's Playbook

THE PRAYER'S PLAYBOOK

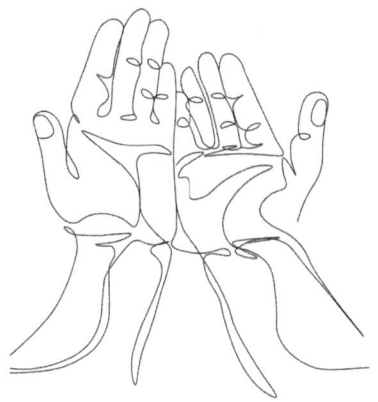

AMARA KURSHA

Duluth, GA

The Prayer's Playbook
Copyright © 2024 Amara Kursha

All rights reserved.

No part of this book may be reproduced or transmitted in any form or by any means, electronic or mechanical, including photocopying, recording or by any information storage and retrieval system, without written permission from the publisher, except for the inclusion of brief quotations in a review.

Address inquiries to the publisher:
The Word Herd
P.O. Box 956324
Duluth, GA 30095

Learn more about the author at:
www.thewordherd.com

ISBN: 978-0-9990909-4-7 (print)
ISBN: 978-0-9990909-5-4 (ebook)

Library of Congress Control Number: 2024925695

Editing and Composition: Annette Purkiss Johnson

Printed in the United States of America

To the champions, either well known or yet discovered. Love God with all your heart, for He'll give you strength and keep you covered.

Contents

Vision 17
DAWG 21
Distress 25
One Shot 29
Perform 33
Dollar Bill 37
Checklist 41
Championship = Partnership 45
The Good Fight 49
Leaders 53
The Underdog 57
Personal 61
Show Out 65
Fruit 69
Jersey 73
Recover 77
G.O.A.T 81
Enjoy 85
Defense 89
All In 93
Fair Play 97
Overtime 101

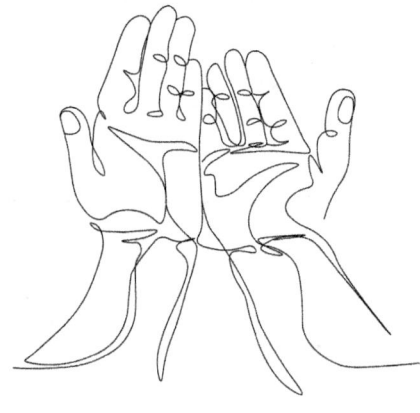

Preface

There is immense power at the core of competition. We see it everywhere—from the commercials on television to the stores where we shop, in schools, sports, workplaces, and on a larger scale, at events like the 2024 Paris Olympics. In this competitive arena, there are winners and losers. As a people, we thrive on the emotions tied to winning, as well as the pain that accompanies losing. One day, you may be celebrated as the best of the best; the next, no one may remember your name. It's an ongoing cycle, and the energy that stems from competition can elevate you to great heights or plunge you to the depths of despair. Thus, we must ask: "How does one stay grounded amidst such turbulence?"

If you have your Bible or Bible app, turn to Hebrews 12:1-3, which reads:

"Therefore, since we are surrounded by such a huge crowd of witnesses to the life of faith, let us strip off every weight that slows us down, especially the sin that so easily trips us up. And let us run with endurance the race God has set before us. We do this by keeping our eyes on Jesus, the champion who initiates and perfects our faith. Because of the joy awaiting Him, He endured the cross, disregarding its shame. Now, He is seated in the place of honor beside God's throne. Think of all the hostility He endured from sinful people; then you won't become weary and give up."
New Living Translation (NLT)

Here, my friends, lies the blueprint for keeping our lives firmly anchored and staying on course. It's neither some elaborate training program nor is it a simple three-step guide to accomplish. It's a mindset shift that allows you to recenter your focus, release your burdens, and keep your eyes on the ultimate prize — Jesus.

I acknowledge that this is easier said than done. When life tosses you in various directions, when people depend on you, and when you yearn to perform your best and succeed, it's incredibly challenging to set aside distractions and focus on Jesus. Yet, it's necessary. Just as horses wear blinders to maintain their focus on the race ahead, God calls us to don our "spiritual blinders" and do the same. This is precisely why **"The Prayer's Playbook"** was written. I recognized a significant need for reminders in sports, work, and other competitive arenas to not just focus on winning but on the One who empowers us to be champions both on earth and for eternity.
As a result, these poems emerged, bringing me great joy as I creatively intertwined the main concepts of competition with the glory of Christ. Drawing from my own experiences and those of others, I realized how easily we can become distracted — whether by the crowd, ego, pride, injury, comparison, adversity, or even family and friends. These distractions can turn a steady race into a turbulent journey in the blink of an eye. Overcoming them begins with what "The Word" instructs us to do first: we must strip ourselves of the added weight they

impose. Of course, we can't ignore injuries, avoid adversity, or eliminate family and friends. However, we can entrust these burdens to God and lay them at His feet. In the poems titled "Distress" and "Perform," I delve into the importance of relinquishing control over these distractions and allowing God to handle them, enabling us to endure the race and pursue our goals.

"**The Prayer's Playbook**" serves as a collection of "spiritual blinders." Each poem is crafted to remind you to stay focused, lighten your load, and keep your eyes on Jesus. There's profound joy in bringing a goal or dream to life, but even greater is achieving that goal with Jesus leading the way. None of this journey was promised to be easy, nor were you meant to walk it alone. In the words of the extraordinary Olympic Champion Sydney McLaughlin-Levrone, "I didn't know what the outcome would be, but I did know He was who I wanted to lead me through the journey." Therefore, seize the spirit of competition, lay your distractions to rest, and let Jesus guide you into the land of victory. Wherever you're ready, ON YOUR MARK, GET SET, AND GO!

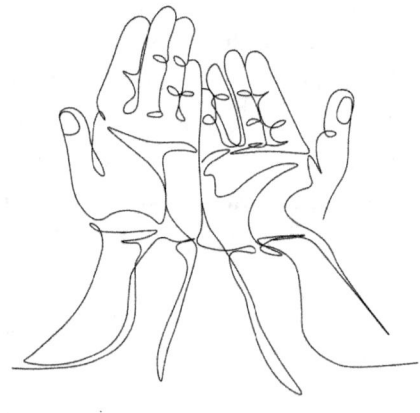

Acknowledgments

With great pleasure, I would like to give honor, glory, praise, and thanks to my Lord and Savior, Jesus Christ for continuously walking with me and gifting me the talent to write. Without Him, I wouldn't have had the strength, creativity, or desire to inspire others in this way. Writing poetry is indeed a unique talent, and through the many opportunities He has delivered me through, I can truly consider myself blessed. I do not take this gift lightly, and I am so grateful that He chose me. Creating this collection with Him at the heart of each poem was something special, and I will never forget the impact His presence had on me as I wrote this book. I pray that His presence is felt among the pages by anyone who decides to pick up this collection and read.

Secondly, I would like to give a very special thanks to the Norcross High School Football Team and the Fellowship of Christian Athletes, who have invited me on numerous occasions to recite poems to their players and coaches. Because my poetry is geared specifically toward athletics and their mission to keep Jesus at the forefront of their programs, the astounding encouragement and feedback from the student-athletes, honestly, inspired me to create this book for many more to see. On a weekly basis, mainly during football season, I go before the players and share a poem to get them excited about the game ahead and to keep their spirits and faith high before it's time to lock in and get focused. Outside of the immediate reactions and snaps of approval, I typically receive a report back from the school's chaplain, who also happens to be my pastor. The reports are always positive and heartening to hear, especially when the result is a victory on the field. Because of their willingness to listen and their warm welcome, I want to thank them from the bottom of my heart. I wouldn't have been able to reach and touch as many lives as I have with my gift if it were not for them. They make me better.

To my family, thank you for supporting me through thick and thin. You know that I wrote this book during one of the most trying times of my life, and having you by my side made the process both doable and worthwhile. Your constant reminders of how far I've come and your motivation pushed me to complete this book and continue showing up for the players. I'm so blessed to have such a powerful support system, and I wouldn't trade you all for the world. I love you and thank you so much.

Lastly, I would like to thank you, the reader, for your competitive spirit and your interest in reading "The Prayer's Playbook." You holding this book right now is another answered prayer and dream come true. Because of you, I'm one step closer to inspiring a life, changing a life, and, or winning a life for the Kingdom of God. For that, you are greatly appreciated, and I thank you.

Vision

Are you content just standing still,
Or do your goals have room to grow?
You can't achieve your very best
Without a plan to guide the show

First, see it clearly in your mind
Where you are now, and where you'll be
Map out the details with intent,
And craft your future thoughtfully

This isn't just another dream,
But how you'll shape what lies ahead
A glimpse of hope into your future,
The track on which your feet will tread

Whether a rookie or a vet
You need this strategy, a guide
You can't give God nothing to bless
And still expect Him to provide

So, write down your aspirations
And take some time with them to pray
Remember, time won't wait for you
Your future's only steps away

This choice will sculpt your whole career,
It will be your best decision
For we know that people perish,
Because of their lack of vision.

DAWG
......

You all know you have it in you,
Might have to dig a little deep
The thing that keeps you up at night
Tossing and turning in your sleep

Every week a new contender,
The competition gives you drive
Your faith in Christ maintains your hope
And through the fight you feel alive

You stay hungry for the mission,
When you meet fear, you turn the dial
You don't make any excuses
And you still go the extra mile

No one can beat you, but yourself
You're ten toes down and on the grind
And this confidence within you
Cannot be bought, it's hard to find

Every single ounce of effort
With nothing left in you to pour
You must attack every moment
Despite the minutes or the score

Opponents will come against you,
But don't get caught up in the fog
So, when the game is on the line
The question is: "Are you a DAWG?"

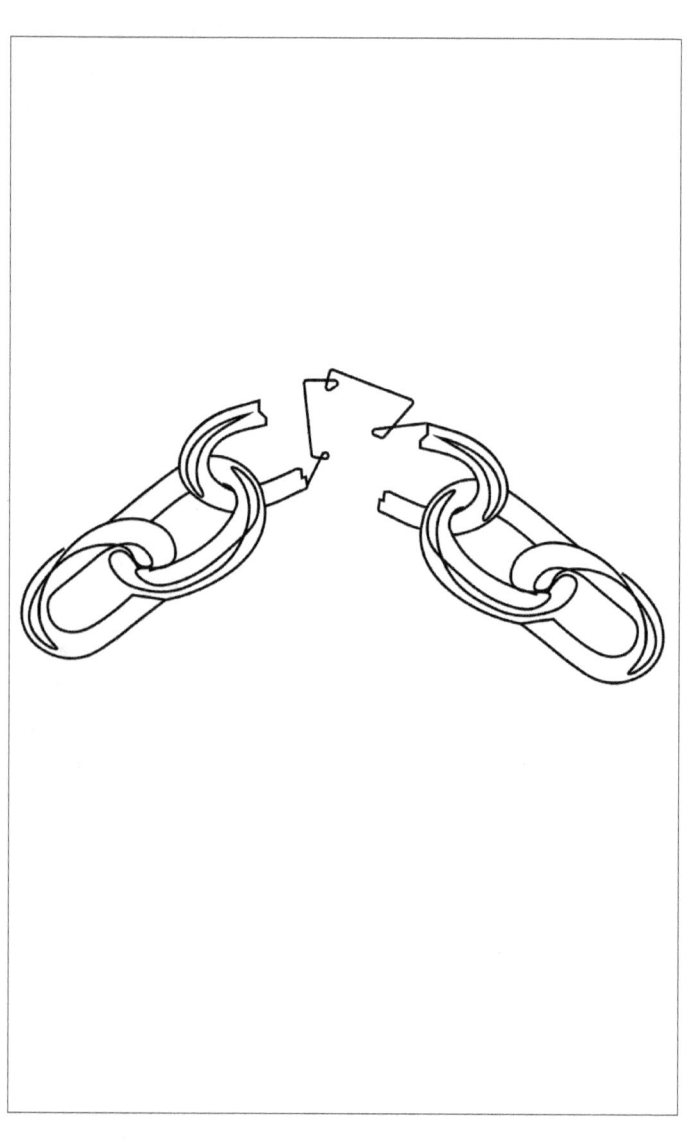

Distress

Not every game will go as planned,
And trouble may invade your home
You try and try but can't break through,
As problems seem to freely roam

But know, your issues aren't the end,
They're just a piece and not the whole
So don't give up beneath the pressure
Release the need to have control

Give it to Him who fights your battles,
Who knows the length, who knows the way
He sees the hurdles on your path,
And gives you strength for each new day

He is the trainer, He's the coach
Not just in sport, but in your life
He asks for trust, for you to lean
On Him, amid your deepest strife

He'll lift you up on eagle's wings,
With love that carries every weight
Then you'll see, none of it was failure,
But instead a play for you to be great

Amara Kursha

In time, success will come to you,
And through your faith, He'll surely bless
So lay it all down at His feet
Your every worry and distress.

One Shot

You're just one thought away from victory
As well, one challenge away from a win
One meaningful prayer from changing your life
And being proud of the person within

In one moment, the crowd screams champion
And one day you can be kissing your ring
Only if two or three of you agree
To have full faith in the gifts that you bring

One big choice may make all the difference
One small play may change the way of the game
You need to believe that you can achieve
Anything you ask for in Jesus' name

Be the leader that your team can count on
Be so relentless one step at a time
Know together that you can make history
And all that it takes is one made up mind

One hope right now is all that should matter
One ambitious heart is all that you need
One beating with purpose, willing to fight,
And to sacrifice for all to succeed

In this life you'll be given some chances,
But sometimes all you'll have is just one shot
So, believe that you can, trust in God's will
Buckle down and give it all that you've got.

Perform

Take a second to relax your shoulders
For upon them both you have placed a weight
Know that the world is not yours to carry
And despite this feeling, that you'll be great

The crowd will not determine your value
Those commentators truly have no say
What matters is the strength that lives inside
And the preparation done for today

Know that those workouts weren't all for nothing
All of your team-building was not in vain
You will exceed all your expectations
And push through every penalty and pain

You're an able child of the Most High God
And with His support your talents will prevail
You're designed in His image and likeness
Therefore, you were never designed to fail

Look to your team because you're not alone
Distribute the workload to get it done
Give it your best with no limitations
And please don't ever forget to have fun

Have faith in yourself and in your Savior
For together you'll weather any storm
Move mountains around any obstacle
And overcome the pressure to perform.

Dollar Bill

If you're only in this thing for money
And you think it will buy you some respect
Please reconsider your true intentions
Because you won't get that from just a check

If you're only here for fame and status
To flaunt and dazzle, to impress,
Know that fortune flickers like a flame
And it can never define your success

If your only motive was to make it
For those you love, who look to feed
Guard well your heart, for soon you'll learn
Their wants may turn from need to greed

Because wealth can bring both best and worst
When there's zeros that's on the line
Some climb in numbers, but find themselves cursed
As their character begins to decline

There's more to life than gold and gain
You're blessed, but don't forget to see
The moment's wealth should not sustain
A sense of false supremacy

So, be humble and wise in your spending
Don't get wrapped up in the flash and the thrill
God gave you this platform for His glory
Not to live and die by the dollar bill.

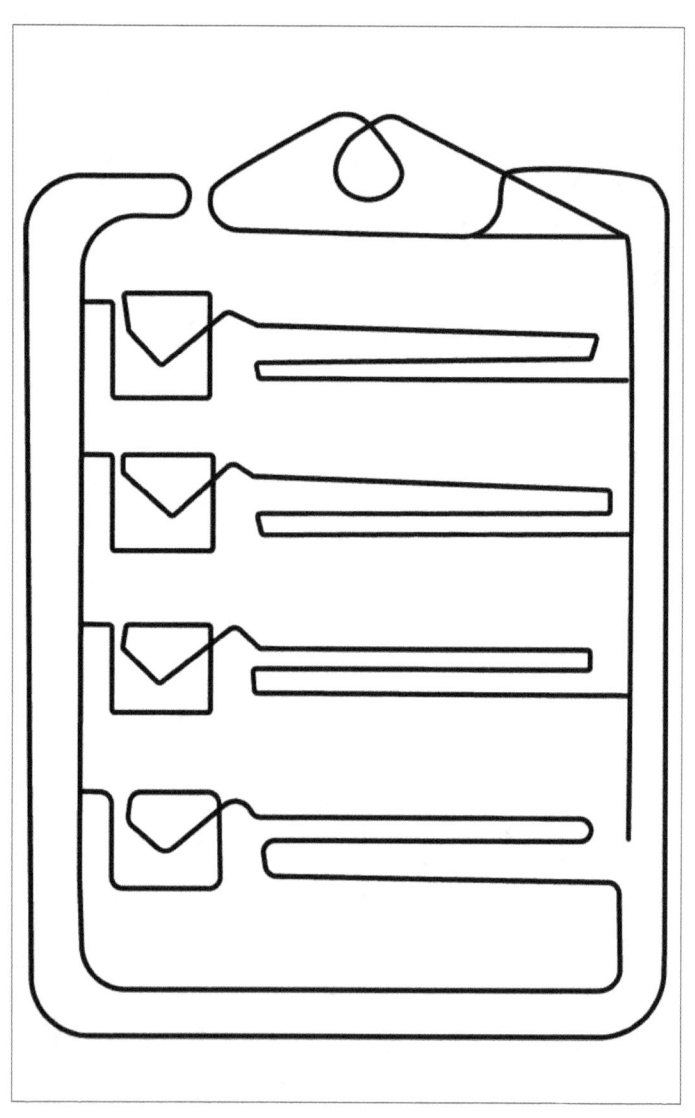

Checklist

What time do you rise in the morning?
What do you often choose to feed your mind?
How healthy are your daily decisions?
Is your integrity well-defined?

You have some people depending on you
On and off the track, the court or field
And no matter if you like it or not
What's important to you will be revealed

You will never get to pick who's watching
So, be the example you want to see
Create balance in life, find your own way,
And embrace your responsibility

First, make sure you've crafted a schedule.
Prioritize prayer as part of your day
For neglecting your faith or dreams for cash,
Isn't worth what the world has to pay

You said that you want to be successful
But success comes with a hefty price
It's time, hard work, and a mind that won't rest,
With discipline and a lot of sacrifice

So, handle the tasks that need to be done,
Be wise in your actions, strive and persist
Get your priorities set in order
And one by one check them off of your list.

Championship = Partnership

Championships are won by organizations
No victory comes from a one-man show
Each role is integral for all to succeed
And your position, positions others to grow

Trust that your coaches aren't out to get you
They've been appointed to execute the plan
Believe that God gives them the wisdom to win
So commit and help them out where you can

Your captains are chosen victory leaders
Listen, observe, then act when it's your turn
Identify your strengths and weaknesses
And as a team, humbly take time to learn

Then as a unit you'll come to form one body
Together as one team, one dream, and one sound
From the owners, players and even water boys
You're all fighting on the same battleground

Remember, any wounds will affect the body
And unchanged attitudes will shift your career
Your communication will be the cornerstone
Which will totally make or break the atmosphere

Please stand by and listen to one another
Keep hearts focused and faithful to the Lord
See that you're all so deep into a partnership
And all you need is everyone to be on board.

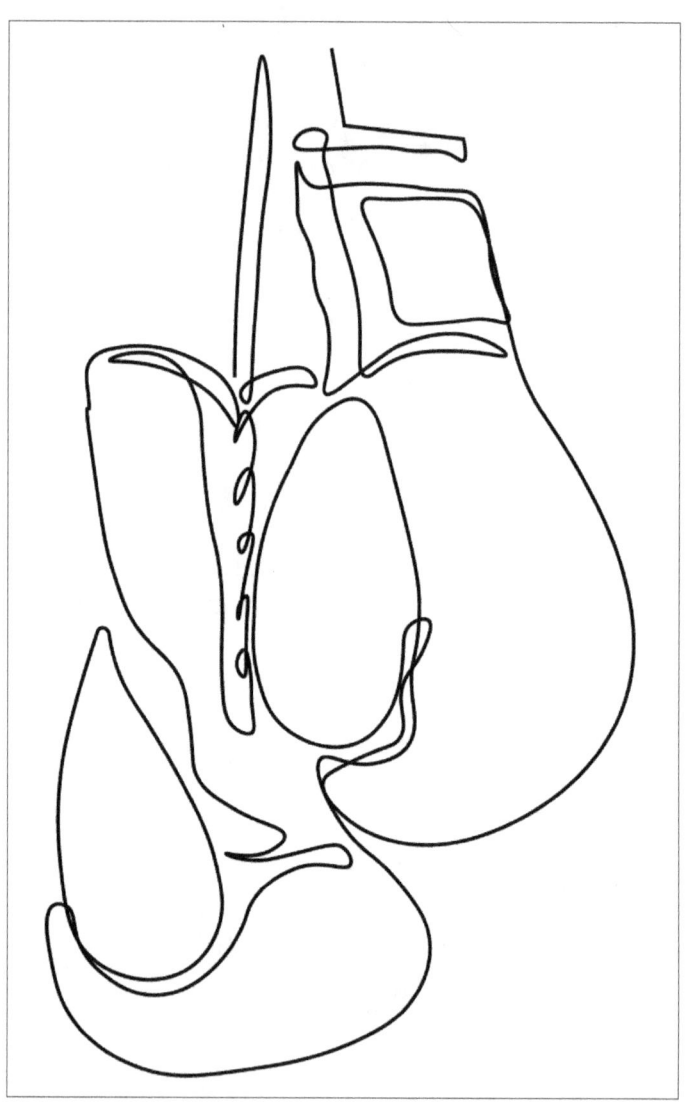

The Good Fight

He never said it would be easy,
This game of life we're called to play,
But He shows us that it's worth it,
As we walk in purpose day by day

Each morning brings a brand-new blessing,
Every problem's just a seed
Planted deep within His truth,
To yield the fruit of what we need

He's faithfully right by your side,
Much closer than your closest friend
He's got your back just like a coat,
His love's unbroken, without end

There'll be days of grueling training,
With sweat that drips down from your brow,
And heaviness within your heart,
With questions lingering, asking how?

But faith will be the force that drives you,
For you know His love is true,
Strong enough to lift you higher,
Through all the pain that you push through

Amara Kursha

And when the storm begins to part,
You'll see His glory shining bright,
Because you gave your very all,
And chose to fight the good fight.

Leaders

Some players are simply built different
With a mindset designed to pursue
They hunt for ways they can breed success
And lead from the front with a vision in view

They're the first to step up and take action
The ones you turn to for advice
You'll never catch them complaining or stuck
They stay on the move, calm and precise

They don't get down when the load is heavy
Because these players stay excited
Fueled by God and their own potential
They work their craft, forever ignited

They have the drive to become true winners
And maximize every skill they wield
They may fall down, but they get back up
Pushing through each challenge on the field

They know encouragement is vital
They know their worth and what they deserve
They understand their role on the team
And the best position is to serve

They know their power and choose to give
As light-bearers and hope feeders
Essential guides along the journey
We call them teammates and our leaders

The Underdog

"No, you're just not good enough,"
That's what the fools and haters say
They never saw you coming up,
But you made it here anyway

You twisted up their spiteful words,
And turned their hate to motivation
You flipped the script, refused to quit,
And showed them through your preparation

You're not the one to play with,
For you were chosen for this thing
And with God standing with you,
You're stepping closer to that ring

You've learned to block the noisy doubt,
The words they used to tear you down
You pray in silence, finding strength,
To rise above and claim your crown

You're much better than you think,
And don't you worry if you're small
Some opponents may be bigger,
But even most giants are known to fall

Amara Kursha

So now it's time, no more delay,
Run full speed, don't slow to jog
Armor up, with purpose clear,
And shock the world as the underdog.

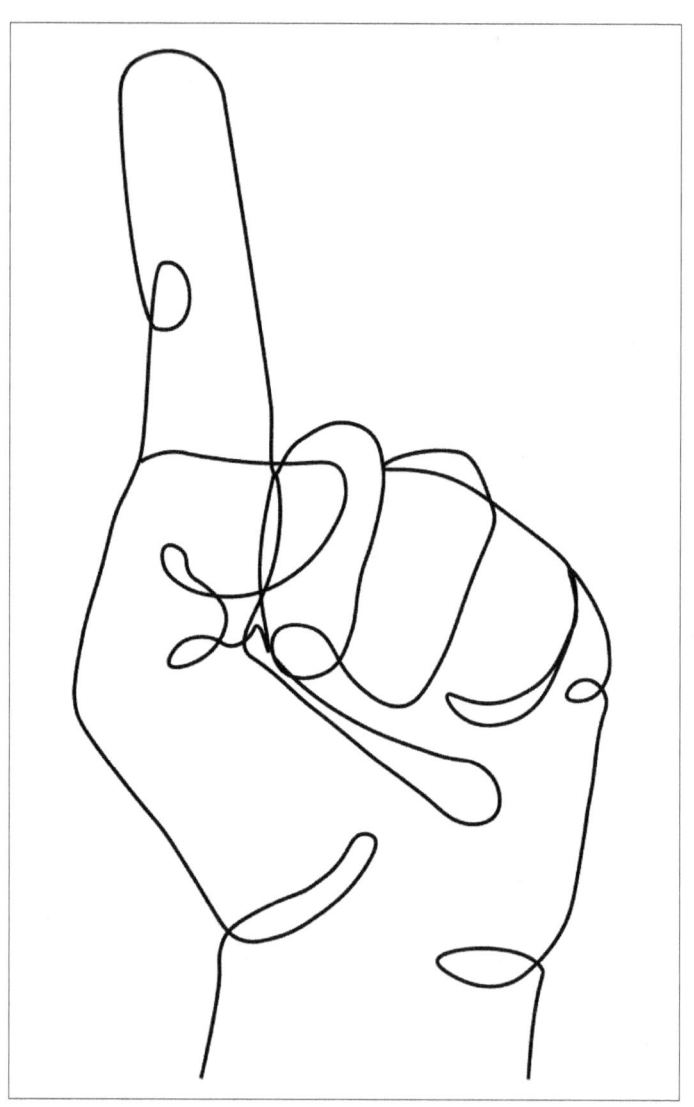

Personal

So, you've been knocked down, doubted,
They treat you like you're just a joke
Equipped, but still they overlook,
And judged before you even spoke

They say, "Don't buy into the hype,"
They claim your talents are a fluke
But deep inside, you know your worth
A faith they'd never dare rebuke

Just know you're in good company,
For Jesus faced the same disdain
They spat, they mocked, and crucified,
Hoping He'd bow His head in shame

But they knew nothing of His power,
Nor the impact He would achieve
He did the most unexpected thing
He held on strong, chose to believe

You know exactly what you seek,
The purpose burning in your soul
So, turn the tables, stand your ground,
And like your Savior, just be bold

Far more than empty, foolish talk,
You're outstanding and versatile
You know it's about team business,
But this one here is personal.

Show Out

You think that you're dependable
And you're the go-to girl or guy
That you do this by your lonesome,
Without another standing by

I suggest you reconsider
And give your side a second glance
For each moment that you're winning,
God's doing His victory dance

He's woven into all your triumphs,
Guiding every step you take
He's there when you lace up your shoes,
And with each effort that you make

No matter what you've accomplished,
It's time you grasp the truth at last:
Without Him, we are not enough,
For He's with us present, future and past

Count your blessings as His glory
And your success, the work of grace
Without Him, you'd be standing still,
But with Him, you're dancing in first place

You might appear to be the hero,
But we now know without a doubt
That behind everything we do,
God's showing up and showing out.

Fruit
. . . . .

As a player, you have potential
That's firmly planted in the ground
And what you do will then determine
How well your growth will come around

Your team will serve as your protection
Your consistency will be your light,
Your attitude will become your water
And faith will nourish you day and night

Who you keep around as company
Will sway how deep your roots can grow
They'll either keep you flourishing
Or stunt the progress you worked to show

And if you make it through the season
You'll see the buds begin to sprout
The product of your perseverance
Unfazed by drought or lingering doubt

Yet, the quality of your results,
Will not be from hype or outward shine
It will be measured by your spirit
In how you live with truth aligned

Most people will not remember you
By your money, your cars, or your pursuit
In the end, none of that will matter
For you'll be remembered by your fruit

So, if you find yourself facing problems
Look inside, down deep and you'll discover
You have all that it takes to overcome
And come back stronger, when you recover

Recover

Sometimes we think that we're invincible
And from this reality we detach
We think that we're built to conquer the world
And come out every time without a scratch

In truth, we must all be realistic
Each day, as we cover ourselves in prayer
Though we work for weeks and months on end
Our bodies will encounter wear and tear

For some, our ankles will twist and buckle
Sprains need a wrap, taped tight and secure
Sometimes we face more than just bruises
Ligaments torn, with breaks to endure

Yet there's no need to live in great fear
For our gracious Lord, is a living shield
Not one injury can stop your purpose
Plus, by faith and His stripes you can be healed

Whatever the ailment, you can treat it
You'll have the strength to restore your core
Stay focused, do what's required of you
To be healthier than ever before

Jersey
. . . .

Today who are you fighting for?
Is it for you or for the crowd?
Whose approval are you seeking?
Who do you want to make most proud?

Are you out here for your rivals?
Why do you even break a sweat?
Are you fulfilled with all this work?
Do you live each day with regret?

You must choose to work with purpose
Before your training feels mundane
Walk in love, not obligation
That leads to going quite insane

This is not a little hobby
You're here for such a time as this
Be the change and be a blessing
So real, the world cannot dismiss

Get with God and ask some questions
Learn yourself through self-reflection
Find out exactly where you stand
For a good sense of direction

None of your work will be in vain
Continue to play, right on track
For the Lord, who lives in your heart
And for the jersey that's on your back

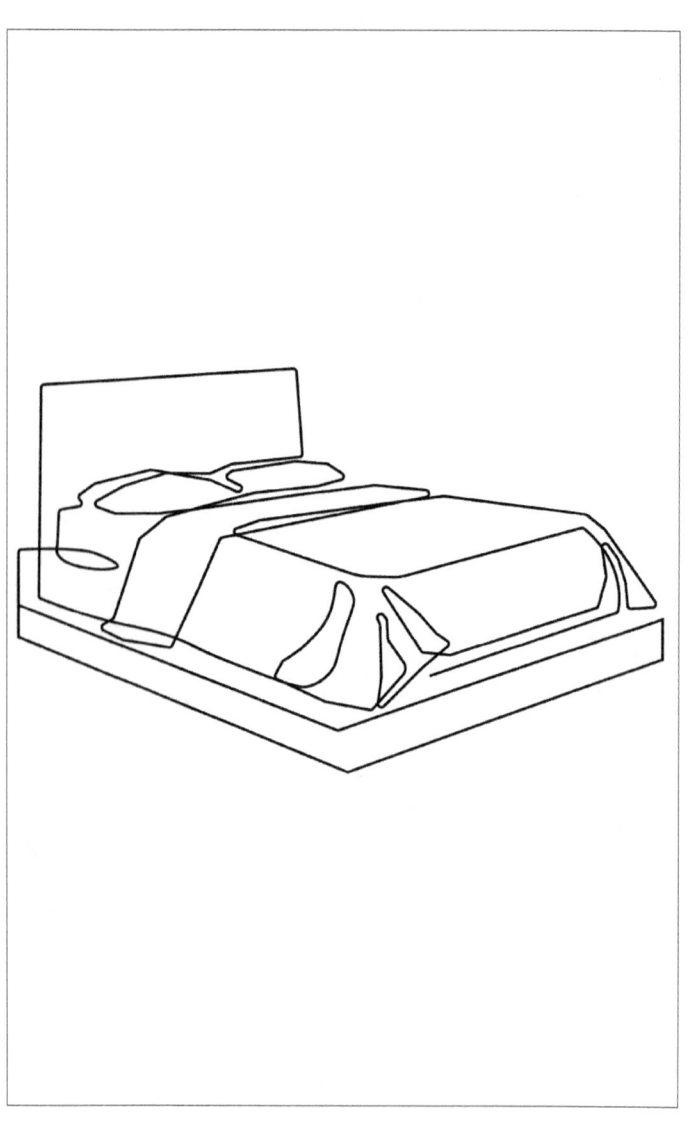

G.O.A.T

I know we all have our favorite player
The one we'd argue for and go to bat
We know their family, friends, their cars and clothes
And their performance down to every stat

Do we have that same exact energy,
For the One who never played a game?
Never won a ring, but He's the King of Kings
And His sacrifice worth the Hall of Fame

If you could buy, would you wear His jersey
Be in the crowd with His name on your back
Cheering loud for the Heavens to hear you speak
With no fears of your peers giving you flack?

Does He come up in the conversation
When you're speaking of ranks and all who's great?
Isn't it clear to see, across the board
That His position isn't up for debate?

You can have those to whom you look up
But be wise to not make them an idol
Don't study them more than you do His Word
And loosely give this overused title

He is our God who is over all things
He is the same and always in His prime
Other people may be spectacular
But He is truly the *Greatest of All Time*

Enjoy

You may be going through the motions
And sick and tired of having to wait
But you cannot rush what's meant for you
Especially if you want to be great

In due time you will reap your harvest
Yet for right now, you have to work and grind
Keep your eyes fixed on the road ahead,
And leave your worries and doubts behind

It won't remain like this forever,
For someday soon you will get your chance
And even when it seems uncertain,
You can still praise the Lord in advance

Ups and downs are a part of the journey,
Don't take for granted what you could learn
Take notes for those who come after,
And think of the blessings you'll get in return

It isn't all about emotions,
They sway and shift just like the breeze
The prize you long for, day by day,
Comes to those whose faith doesn't cease

Amara Kursha

So do not fret about the timing
In fact, that attitude you need to destroy
Sit back and ride out your destiny
And let the process be something you enjoy

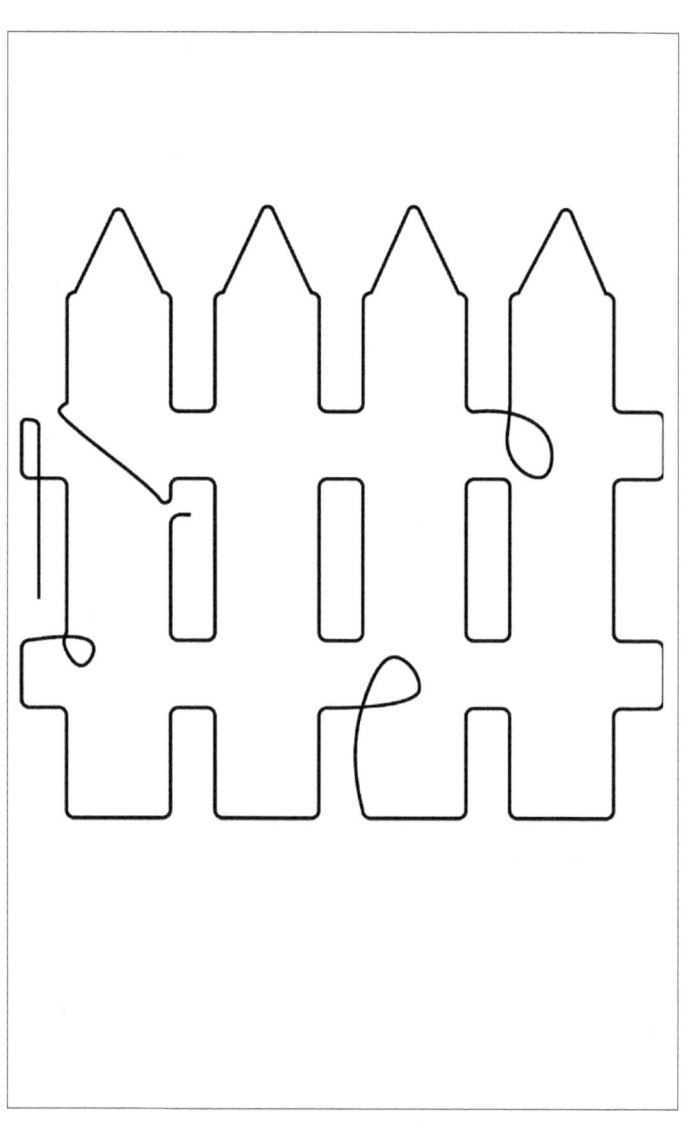

Defense

From the moment that you open your eyes
The enemy lurks, waiting to bombard
Your thoughts, your flesh, all your plans for the day
That's why you must always keep up your guard

Protect first, your greatest investments
Your body, your mind, and your heart
Stand firm in the wisdom of the Word of God
To shield yourself from each fiery dart

For doubt can slip in without warning,
And make you question if God's on your side
Deception can twist you and lead you astray
When temptation and purpose collide

As long as he's keeping you distracted
You're out of the game, accepting defeat
Delaying the blessings meant just for you
And being discouraged to even compete

So be prepared, put on your full armor
Equip yourself with faith, and speak the Word
Deny all attempts to destroy your peace
And refuse to let your prayers go unheard

Amara Kursha

Stray away from being disconnected
Living in a cycle that makes no sense
Learn the enemy's ways and trust in God
To build a strong and solid defense

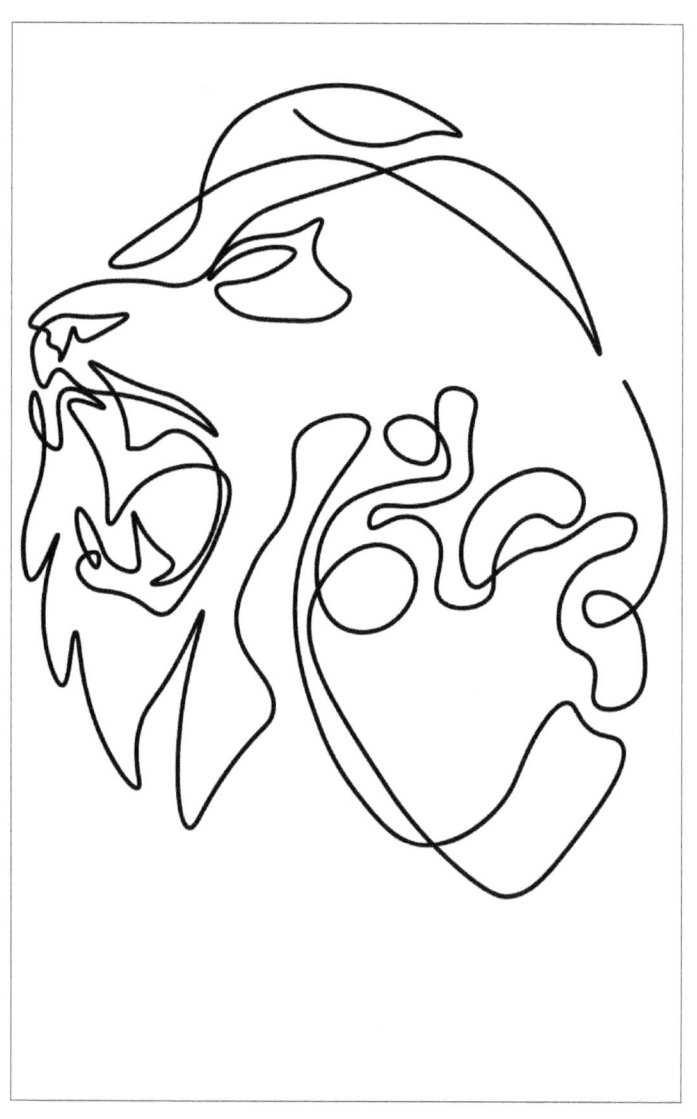

All In
· · · · ·

Tell me, are you totally committed?
Or is it just your big toe that's in the water?
You have been molded and crafted to play
But how you perform isn't up to the potter

You claim that you want to be successful
Yet that comes from your center, not from the edge
You can't be straddling the fence of faith
And not expect your success to be on the ledge

Believe in yourself and all your power
To make a difference with what you do
And trust when you give it your best
People will be blessed for you seeing it through

Be the example you wish to inspire
A beacon of hope for believers to seek
The heart of a lion, unafraid to fight
Facing any challenge that threatens the weak

You owe it to yourself and your team
If you're sincere about being a team player
So say what you mean and do what you say
To display your devotion layer by layer

A bit of sacrifice will be required
If it's your desire and your will to win
You can't step in with a hesitant heart
You have to decide and be fully ALL IN

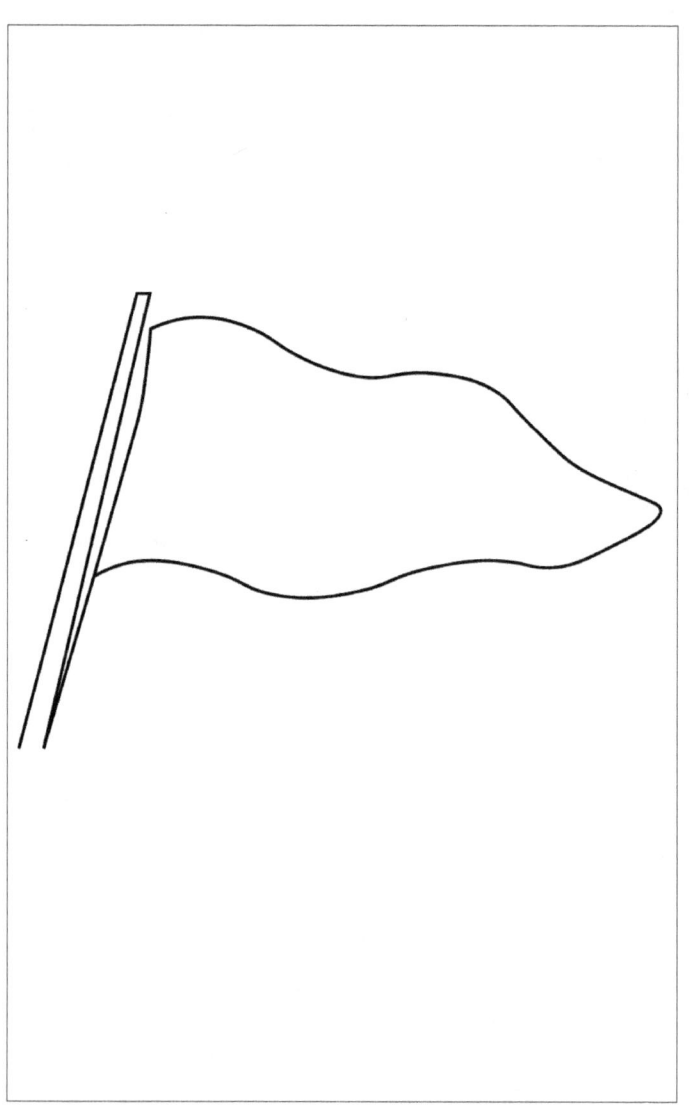

Fair Play

There's a set of rules and unwritten laws
That every player should know and abide
Your ego sometimes gets the best of you
But for this, you have to put it aside

You're not the only one chasing your dreams
So why would you aim to take a cheap shot?
Putting the lives of others in danger
Won't get you any closer to the top

Go drop your pride for some integrity
And justly put a trophy on your shelf
If you think cheating will get you respect
You're not cheating them, but cheating yourself

God truly wants to give you blessings
But you must treat His children right
Congratulate your brothers and sisters
Not acting out of jealousy or spite

You would want to be treated with honor
And be commended for the work you do
Don't be like the world that's living in hate
Do for others what you would want for you

So go out and put your best foot forward
Play your heart out with a touch of care
And you will know that if you're triumphant
You earned every bit of it fair and square

Overtime

You will not always have this moment
You need to think ahead to what lies beyond
It can be ten years or maybe five
But you need to know how you will respond

This position isn't your final stop
There is abundance outside of your sport
Build all you can while you're in this space
And don't be afraid to ask for support

Don't think of yourself as a failure
Just because life shifted to a new gear
Start applauding the work that you've done
For there's no permanence in a career

God knows the plans that He has for you
Believe in your future and in that hope
See that this season is just a fraction
And not your life in its entire scope

Explore and find new opportunities
In places and faces you've yet to know
You'll be amazed by your own ambitions
And how much your faith and dreams can grow

This will not be the end of the world
Just a transition from valley to climb
A beginning of something better
Trading in your jersey for overtime

www.ingramcontent.com/pod-product-compliance
Lightning Source LLC
Chambersburg PA
CBHW070739020526
44118CB00035B/1619